Popular Australiar Zealand Recipes

A Wide Variety of Flavourful Recipes from the Land of Down-Under - Not Only Yummy but Quick & Easy-to-Prepare!

BY: Nancy Silverman

COPYRIGHT NOTICES

Table of Contents

Introduction

These days, travel is not a very safe option since the pandemic began. Many people who used to travel around the world to experience new cultures and new foods are not doing so anymore. Of course, it certainly does not mean that we cannot get to try foods from around the world from within the comforts of our home kitchens! In this collection, I am bringing you my personal top Australian and New Zealand recipes so that you can get a little bit of these cuisines from your home sweet home! Living in the fast-paced world of today can undoubtedly make having family meals together a bit challenging. To help make this a bit easier for you to accomplish, this is a collection of easy-to-prepare meals. I offer you this recipe collection that will give you a chance to share some new recipes with your loved ones! Discover and enjoy unique cultural cuisines all from the comfort and safety of your own home!

Collection of Popular Australian & New Zealand Recipes

Yogurt Salad Dressing

Here is a popular and quick to prepare salad dressing that you are sure to enjoy!

Prep time: 10 minutes

Cook time: 0 minutes

Servings: 8

Ingredients:

- 2 teaspoons lemon juice
- 1 (8-ounce) container plain low-fat yogurt
- 1 teaspoon fresh parsley, chopped
- 1 teaspoon Dijon-style prepared mustard
- 1 teaspoon fresh chives, chopped

Directions:

Whisk your lemon juice and yogurt in a small-sized bowl until smooth.

Add the parsley, chives, and mustard and stir to combine.

Store the dressing in your fridge until ready to serve.

Nutrition Info:

- Calories: 19
- Cholesterol: 2
- Protein: 5
- Fat: 4
- Sodium: 36
- Carbs: 3

Porcupine Meatballs

Here is a fun and tasty meal to serve to your loved ones that are sure to please!

Prep time: 20 minutes

Cook time: 20 minutes

Servings: 5

Ingredients:

- 1 lb. Lean ground beef
- 1 egg
- ¼ cup Worcestershire sauce
- 2 (10-ounce) cans condensed tomato soup
- ¼ cup instant rice
- 1 teaspoon onion salt
- 1 tablespoon parsley, fresh chopped
- ¼ cup onion, chopped
- ¼ teaspoon ground black pepper

Directions:

In a mixing bowl, combine a heaping tablespoon of soup along with a lightly beaten egg. Mix in the onion, salt, pepper, rice, onion, and parsley. Stir in your ground beef, and combine the mixture with your hands. Shape into meatballs about 1 ½ inches round.

Coat a large skillet with some cooking spray, and place over medium heat. Cook your meatballs in a skillet until they are brown on all sides.

Mix the Worcestershire and remaining soup in a bowl until smooth. Scoop mixture over the meatballs. Add a lid to skillet and simmer for about 30 minutes, stirring occasionally. Serve and enjoy!

Nutrition Information:

- Calories: 408
- Fat: 6
- Protein: 6
- Cholesterol: 105
- Carbs: 4

Thai Coconut Chicken

Savour this flavourful dish that has a spicy and pleasing taste you are sure to enjoy!

Prep time: 10 minutes

Cook time: 20 minutes

Servings: 4

Ingredients:

- 3 cups water
- 1 ½ lb. Chicken breasts,
- boneless and skinless, cubed
- 2 cups dry jasmine rice
- 2 cups asparagus, 1-inch pieces
- 1 cup snow peas
- 1 tablespoon curry powder
- 1 cup green onions, chopped
- 1 (14-ounce) can light coconut milk
- ½ cup carrots, shredded

Directions:

Mix your water and rice in a saucepan. Place over high heat, cover and bring to a boil. Once the boil has been reached, lower the heat to a low heat setting and simmer for 20 minutes.

Mix the chicken and curry powder in a bowl, tossing to coat.

Spray a non-stick skillet with cooking spray. Add the chicken to skillet and cook for 4 minutes over medium-high heat, mixing often. Add in the carrots, green onions, snow peas, and asparagus. Continue to cook, add coconut milk, continue to cook until the chicken is thoroughly cooked. Serve hot cooked rice and enjoy!

Nutrition Information:

- Calories: 697
- Fat: 1
- Protein: 9
- Carbs: 4
- Cholesterol: 99

Watermelon Salad

A perfect dish to serve your guests on one of those hot summer days!

Prep time: 30 minutes

Cook time: 0 minutes

Servings: 6

Ingredients:

- 2 quarts of watermelon, seeded and cubed
- ¾ cup red onion, thinly sliced
- 1 tablespoon lime juice, fresh
- ¾ cup feta cheese, crumbled
- 1 cup fresh mint, chopped
- ½ cup black olives, pitted and halved
- 2 tablespoons olive oil

Directions:

In a bowl, add lime juice, along with onion slices, allow to sit for about 10 minutes. The acid will lessen the raw onion flavour from the lime.

In a large bowl, carefully combine your watermelon cubes, mint, onions with lime, black olives, and feta cheese. Drizzle salad with olive oil and toss until well blended. Serve and enjoy!

Nutrition Information:

- Calories: 157
- Fat: 10
- Carbs: 8
- Cholesterol: 17
- Protein: 4

Auzzie-Style Potato & Spinach Frittata

The perfect dish to offer your guests on a roasting hot day!

Prep time: 10 minutes

Cook time: 20 minutes

Servings: 6

Ingredients:

- 6 eggs
- 2 tablespoons olive oil
- 1/3 cup milk
- ½ cup cheddar cheese, shredded
- 2 tablespoons green onions, sliced
- 1 cup spinach, fresh and torn
- 6 red potatoes, sliced
- 1 teaspoon garlic, crushed
- sea salt & black ground pepper, as needed

Directions:

Set your skillet over medium heat setting, add olive oil, add your potatoes to the skillet, and keep covered. Allow the potatoes to cook until soft but still firm; this process should take about 10 minutes.

Add the green onions, spinach, and garlic into the skillet. Season with salt and pepper. Continue to cook until your spinach has wilted; this should take about 2 minutes.

In a bowl, whip the eggs and milk. Add mixture to the skillet over the vegetables. Sprinkle the top with cheddar cheese shreds. Simmer for about 7 minutes or until the eggs become firm. Serve and enjoy!

Nutrition Information

- Calories: 281
- Fat: 1
- Cholesterol: 197
- Carbs: 7
- Protein: 5

Sugar Snap Peas & Mint

Here is a lovely savoury dish to serve on a day when you are looking for a light filling meal!

Prep time: 7 minutes

Cook time: 5 minutes

Servings: 4

Ingredients:

- 3 green onions, chopped
- 2 teaspoons olive oil
- ¾ lb. Sugar snap peas, trimmed
- 1 clove garlic, chopped
- sea salt & black ground pepper, as needed
- 1 tablespoon mint, fresh chopped

Directions:

In a pan, heat your oil, then add the garlic, sugar snap peas, green onion, salt and pepper. Stir the mixture often for about 5 minutes.

Remove the pan from heat, then stir in the mint leafs. Serve and enjoy!

Nutrition Information:

- Calories: 67
- Fat: 4
- Sodium: 75
- Carbs: 3
- Protein: 3

Cantaloupe Spinach Salad & Mint

Have a healthy meal that is great and is easy to prepare!

Prep time: 15 minutes

Cook time: 0 minutes

Servings: 2

Ingredients:

- 1 cup cantaloupe, peeled and cubed
- 4 cups spinach, fresh, chopped
- 1 avocado, sliced
- 1 tablespoon mint apple jelly
- 2 tablespoons mint leafs, fresh chopped
- 3 tablespoons vegetable oil
- 1 ½ teaspoon white wine vinegar
- 1 clove garlic, minced
- ½ cup red bell pepper, diced

Directions:

Add the spinach to serving plates. Divide avocado evenly between plates. Add cantaloupe evenly to each serving plate.

Top each portion with fresh mint leafs and diced red bell pepper.

Mix the white wine vinegar, oil, garlic, and mint jelly in a small bowl. Lightly pour mixture over salads. Serve and enjoy!

Nutrition Information:

- Calories: 376
- Fat: 7
- Carbs: 7
- Protein: 4
- Sodium: 67

Carrot & Spinach Quiche

Enjoy a marvelous light, healthy dish that you can whip up in no time at all!

Prep time: 10 minutes

Cook time: 30 minutes

Servings: 6

Ingredients:

- 6 eggs
- 1 tablespoon olive oil
- 1 onion, diced
- 2 cups Monterey Jack cheese, shredded
- ½ cup carrots, shredded
- 2 (10-ounce) packages of frozen spinach, chopped and thawed
- ½ teaspoon crushed red pepper flakes
- 2 (9-inch) pie crusts
- sea salt & black ground pepper, as needed
- 1/8 teaspoon nutmeg, ground

Directions:

Preheat the grill to a high heat setting.

In a skillet, heat your olive oil on the grill, add onions and cook them until they are soft.

Add the spinach, garlic, and carrots to skillet and continue to cook until there is no liquid left from the spinach.

Remove your skillet from heat, then stir in the eggs and cheese.

Add the nutmeg, red pepper, salt and pepper to taste.

Divide your mixture evenly between the two pie crusts.

Place the pies on the grill and cook for 30 minutes or until a toothpick placed in the middle of the quiche comes out clean. Serve and enjoy!

Nutrition Information:

- Calories: 184
- Fat: 4
- Cholesterol: 82
- Protein: 8
- Carbs: 8

Lemon Artichoke Pesto

A perfect meal to serve that is healthy and tasty and is ready in no time!

Prep time: 15 minutes

Cook time: 0 minutes

Servings: 8

Ingredients:

- ½ cup Parmesan cheese, grated
- ¼ cup cilantro, fresh chopped
- 4 tablespoons lemon juice
- 1 cup walnuts
- ½ cup olive oil
- 1 (8-ounce) package frozen artichokes, chopped and thawed
- ½ teaspoon cayenne pepper
- sea salt to taste
- ½ canola oil

Directions:

In your food processor, pulse your olive oil, canola oil, salt, cayenne pepper, walnuts, garlic, lemon juice, and cilantro until smooth.

Add the mixture to a large bowl. Stir in the Parmesan cheese and chopped artichoke slowly. Serve and enjoy!

Nutrition Information:

- Calories: 386
- Fat: 2
- Protein: 7
- Carbs: 2
- Cholesterol: 6

Pumpkin Stew

A personal favourite of mine, this pumpkin stew will warm you up in no time!

Prep time: 20 minutes

Cook time: 3 ½ hours

Servings: 8

Ingredients:

- 2 ½ lbs. Beef stew meat, sliced into 1-inch cubes
- 4 large potatoes, peeled and cubed
- 1 cup water
- 3 tablespoons vegetable oil, divided
- 4 carrots, sliced
- 1 onion, chopped
- 1 large green bell pepper, diced
- 4 garlic cloves, minced
- sea salt & black ground pepper, as needed
- 1 (14.5-ounce) can whole peeled tomatoes, chopped
- 1 sugar pumpkin
- 2 tablespoons beef bouillon granules

Directions:

Over medium-high heat setting, heat 2 tablespoons of oil in a large stockpot. Add your beef to the pot and cook until meat has browned evenly. Stir in the potatoes, onion, carrots, garlic, green bell pepper, water, salt and pepper. Lower heat and simmer for 3 hours.

Dissolve the beef bouillon in the beef mixture and stir in the tomatoes.

Preheat your oven to 325° Fahrenheit.

Slice the top of the pumpkin off, and discard the pulp and seeds. Add your pumpkin to a heavy baking pan. Transfer your beef mixture inside your pumpkin. Spread the remaining oil over the outside of your pumpkin.

Bake for 2 hours or until tender. For each serving, scrape out some of the pumpkin meat and serve with stew from the pumpkin. Serve hot and enjoy!

Nutrition Information:

- Calories: 592
- Fat: 9
- Carbs: 9
- Cholesterol: 76
- Protein: 4

Sesame Pasta Chicken Salad

The perfect meal to serve on a roasting hot day that is sure to please your lunch guests!

Prep time: 15 minutes

Cook time: 10 minutes

Servings: 8

Ingredients:

- 4 cups chicken breast meat, shredded
- 1/3 cup rice vinegar
- ½ cup vegetable oil
- 1 (16-ounce) package of bow tie pasta
- 1/3 cup light soy sauce
- 1 teaspoon sesame oil
- ¼ cup sesame seeds
- ½ teaspoon ginger, ground
- 3 tablespoons white sugar
- 1/3 cup cilantro, fresh chopped
- 1/3 cup green onion, chopped
- sea salt & black ground pepper, as needed

Nutrition Information:

- Calories: 349
- Fat: 2
- Carbs: 24
- Protein: 9

Sweet Potato, Pumpkin & Leek Soup

A hearty and flavourful soup that your entire family is sure to enjoy!

Prep time: 12 minutes

Cook time: 1 hour and 10 minutes

Servings: 8

Ingredients:

- 4 sweet potatoes, peeled and diced
- 4 tablespoons olive oil
- 3 leeks, chopped
- 1 white onion, diced
- 1 carrot, shredded
- 1 stalk celery, chopped
- 2 tablespoons garlic, chopped
- 1 sugar pumpkin, seeded and cubed
- 1 cup heavy whipping cream
- 1 bay leaf
- 1-quart chicken stock
- 1 tablespoon sage, fresh chopped
- 1 dash ground nutmeg
- 1 dash ground cloves
- 1 dash ground cinnamon
- sea salt & black ground pepper, as needed

Directions:

Add your oil to a heavy bottom pot and place over medium heat setting. Add the sweet potatoes, garlic, pumpkin, carrot, onion, leeks, and celery. Sauté your veggies until they have browned.

Add your bay leaf, cream, and stock to the pot. Bring mixture to a boil. Lower heat setting to low and simmer for an hour, or until the veggies are tender.

Add the cinnamon, nutmeg, sage, cloves along with salt and pepper for seasoning. Remove the bay leaf and blend. Serve hot and enjoy!

Nutrition Information:

- Calories: 252
- Fat: 5
- Cholesterol: 41
- Carbs: 26
- Protein: 8

Roasted Red Pepper & Crab Soup

A yummy treat for the seafood lovers out there that is sure to please!

Prep time: 15 minutes

Cook time: 1 hour

Servings: 6

Ingredients:

- 1 lb. Crab meat, cooked and flaked
- 6 red bell peppers, seeded and sliced into quarters
- 1 large potato, peeled and chopped
- ¼ teaspoon cayenne pepper
- 1-quart half-and-half cream
- 1 (32-ounce) carton of chicken broth
- sea salt, as needed
- ½ teaspoon garlic powder
- ½ teaspoon basil, dried

Directions:

Preheat your oven's broiler for 5 minutes.

Place your red peppers with skin side up on a broiler pan. Allow to broil until the skins turn black. Place peppers into a bowl and cover with a brown paper bag; this allows them to steam to loosen the skins. The process takes about 10 minutes.

Once the skins have loosened, remove and dispose of them. Add the cut roasted peppers into a pan along with chicken broth and chopped potatoes. Boil mixture over high heat and add garlic powder, basil, cayenne pepper, half-and-half, and salt.

Bring back to boil, then lower heat and simmer for 45 minutes

Once the potatoes are tender, add your soup to a blender and puree until smooth. Add the pureed soup to a saucepan and add in the crab. Heat over medium heat setting for about 5 minutes or until warm. Serve and enjoy!

Nutrition Information:

- Calories: 352
- Fat: 8
- Carbs: 5
- Cholesterol: 121
- Protein: 7

Corned Beef & Cabbage

A savoury and healthy dish that will make you feel satisfied and energized!

Prep time: 20 minutes

Cook time: 3 ½ hours

Servings: 6

Ingredients:

- 1 head cabbage, cored and coarsely chopped
- 1 (3 lb.) corned beef brisket, along with spice packet
- 6 potatoes, peeled and cubed
- 1 (1.5 fluid ounce) Irish whiskey

Directions:

Add the beef brisket and spice packet to a large pot and add enough water to cover. Bring brisket to a boil, then reduce heat to low and simmer for 2 hours.

Add the potatoes and cabbage and continue to simmer for an additional 1 ½ hour. Stir in the whiskey when it is nearly done.

Serve hot and enjoy!

Nutrition Information:

- Calories: 360
- Fat: 4
- Carbs: 8
- Cholesterol: 73
- Protein: 7

Lobster Tails Steamed in Beer

A delightful treat for all of the seafood lovers that is quick and easy to prepare!

Prep time: 5 minutes

Cook time: 8 minutes

Servings: 2

Ingredients:

- ½ (12-fluid ounce) beer
- 2 large whole lobster tail

Directions:

Add beer to a saucepan and allow it to boil over a high heat setting.

Cut a slit up the back of the lobster shell along its length.

Place a steamer basket over the saucepan containing boiling beer. Add your thawed lobster tails to the steamer basket and add a cover on top. Lower the heat setting to simmer and cook for about 8 minutes. Serve and enjoy!

Nutrition Information:

- Calories: 209
- Fat: 7
- Cholesterol: 180
- Carbs: 1
- Protein: 1
- Sodium: 566

Seared Tuna & Wasabi Butter Sauce

If you are looking for a savoury, healthy meal to serve, I suggest you give this recipe a try!

Prep time: 5 minutes

Cook time: 35 minutes

Servings: 6

Ingredients:

- 6 (6-ounce) fresh tuna steaks, 1-inch thick
- 2 tablespoons white wine vinegar
- ¼ cup shallots, minced
- 10-fluid ounces white wine
- 1 tablespoon wasabi paste
- 1 cup butter, unsalted, cubed
- 1 tablespoon soy sauce
- 1 cup cilantro leafs, chopped
- sea salt and black pepper, as needed
- 1 tablespoon olive oil

Directions:

In a small saucepan, combine your shallots, white wine vinegar, and white wine over a medium heat setting. Simmer until the liquid in your pan is reduced by about 2 tablespoons.

Strain out the shallots and discard them, pour the liquid back into the pan.

Stir your wasabi and soy sauce into the pan. Whisk in one cube of butter over low heat, allowing your mixture to emulsify. Do not bring the mixture back to boil.

Once the butter is incorporated into the mixture, add the cilantro and remove the pan from heat.

Transfer the mixture into a bowl, then set aside.

In a large skillet over medium heat setting, place tuna steaks after being brushed with olive oil. Now, season your tuna steaks with some salt and pepper.

Place the tuna steaks into the hot skillet, sear each side for about 5 minutes. Do not overcook steaks; there should be a little pink in the center of fish when served. Serve steaks with sauce and enjoy!

Nutrition Information:

- Calories: 533
- Carbs: 5
- Fat: 6
- Cholesterol: 158
- Protein: 7
- Sodium: 278

Lamb Curry

Looking for a dish with a bit of spice to it, then I suggest you give this lamb curry recipe a try!

Prep time: 25 minutes

Cook time: 2 hours

Servings: 6

Ingredients:

- 2 ¼ lbs. Lamb meat, sliced into 1-inch cubes
- curry paste
- 2 teaspoons cumin seeds
- 2 teaspoons coriander seeds
- 5 whole red chile peppers, dried
- 3 tablespoons garlic paste
- 6 curry leafs, fresh
- 2 teaspoons turmeric, ground
- 2 teaspoons ginger paste
- ¼ cup vegetable oil
- ½ cup ghee, melted
- 1 (13.5-ounce) can coconut milk
- 2 cups water, divided
- 4 onion, sliced ¼ inch thick
- 1 teaspoon fennel seeds
- 6 cardamom pods
- 1 teaspoon sugar
- 1 cinnamon stick
- 2 teaspoons garam seeds
- 1 tablespoon tamarind paste
- 3 tablespoons warm water

Directions:

Toast coriander seeds in a pan over low heat settings until they start to pop and brown. Repeat this toasting method with the dried red peppers and cumin seeds.

Add each ingredient into a spice grinder when finished. Add some salt, and grind into a fine powder. Mix with garlic and ginger to make a thick paste.

Sprinkle the lamb with turmeric. Toast the fennel seeds in the same fashion as previous seeds, then set them aside.

Heat a Dutch oven over medium heat with vegetable oil and ghee. Cook your onions for 10 minutes or until golden brown. Mix in the curry paste, then fry for a minute.

Add in the lamb and fry for another minute.

Add 1 cup water along with 2/3 of coconut milk and bring to a boil. Lower the heat setting to low. Simmer for 10 minutes.

Mix in 1 cup water along with a cinnamon stick, toasted fennel seeds, cardamom pods, and leftover coconut milk. Cover leaving the lid ajar, and return to a simmer. Cook mixture for about 1 ½ hour or until lamb is tender. Stir lamb mixture occasionally.

Once the lamb is tender, add in the tamarind paste melted in 3 tablespoons of water, sugar, and garam masala. Cook lamb mixture for an additional 5 minutes or until sauce thickens. Remove the cardamom pods and cinnamon stick. Serve hot and enjoy!

Nutrition Information:

- Calories: 519
- Fat: 1
- Carbs: 2
- Cholesterol: 116
- Protein: 6
- Sodium: 479

Fava Beans & Green Risotto

Savour this easy-to-prepare healthy meal that will leave you feeling satisfied!

Prep time: 25 minutes

Cook time: 25 minutes

Servings: 4

Ingredients:

- 4 cups chicken broth
- ½ lb. Fava beans, fresh and unshelled
- 1 onion, finely chopped
- 3 tablespoons butter, divided
- ¼ cup Parmesan cheese, grated
- 1 cup Arborio rice
- ¼ cup white wine
- sea salt to taste

Directions:

Over medium heat setting, bring salted water to a boil.

Skin the Fava beans and discard the pods. Cook the favas for 4 minutes in boiling water. Drain the beans, and instantly immerse in ice water. Allow beans to cool for about 2 minutes. Pierce the Fava and remove them from their skins by squeezing.

Add ¾ of the Fava beans to your food processor.

In another pan, bring your broth to a simmer, and keep it hot.

In another large pan over medium heat setting, melt 2 tablespoons of butter, add onions, and set low heat. Cook for approximately 5 minutes, then add rice and cook and stir for 2 minutes.

Raise the heat to medium and add the wine; once it is absorbed, add a small amount of hot stock. Once your stock is absorbed, continue to add more and more until the rice is cooked; stir often.

Add the remaining Fava, cheese, 2 tablespoons of butter, and the pureed Fava into the cooked rice. Cook mixture and stir over medium heat until the butter and cheese have melted. Lightly sprinkle with sea salt to season. Serve and enjoy!

Nutrition Information:

- Calories: 457
- Fat: 11.1
- Carbs: 69.5
- Cholesterol: 32
- Protein: 16.5
- Sodium: 1412

Ginger Vegetable Stir Fry

A dish sure to delight all those that are dining at your table!

Prep time: 20 minutes

Cook time: 15 minutes

Servings: 6

Ingredients:

- 2 teaspoons ginger root, fresh chopped, divided
- 1 tablespoon cornstarch
- ¼ cup vegetable oil, divided
- 2 tablespoons soy sauce
- 3 tablespoons water
- ¾ cup carrots, julienned
- ½ cup snow peas
- 2 garlic cloves, minced
- 1 head broccoli, sliced into florets
- ½ cup green beans, halved
- ½ tablespoon sea salt
- ¼ cup onion, chopped

Directions:

In a large bowl, blend ginger, garlic, 2 tablespoons vegetable oil, and cornstarch. Stir in the snow peas, carrots, green beans, and broccoli. Toss lightly to coat.

In a wok, add 2 tablespoons of oil over medium heat setting. Cook the veggie mix for about 2 minutes and stir often.

Mix in the soy sauce and water and leftover ginger, onion, and salt. Cook until the vegetables become tend but yet still crisp. Serve and enjoy!

Nutrition Information:

- Calories: 119
- Fat: 3
- Cholesterol: 0
- Carbs: 8
- Protein: 2
- Sodium: 903

Fish Chowder

A dish that is healthy and tasty that will make for a perfect lunchtime or light dinner meal!

Prep time: 25 minutes

Cook time: 30 minutes

Servings: 8

Ingredients:

- 2 lbs. Of cod, diced into 1/2-inch cubes
- 2 tablespoons butter
- 4 cups chicken stock
- 4 large fresh mushrooms, chopped
- 1 cup clam juice
- 1 stalk celery, diced
- 2 cups onion, chopped
- ½ cup all-purpose flour
- 2 (12-fluid ounce) cans of evaporated milk
- 1/8 teaspoon Old Bay Seasoning
- garnish: cooked crumbled bacon (optional)
- sea salt and black ground pepper, to taste
- 4 cups potatoes, diced

Directions:

Set a stockpot over the medium heat setting, add two tablespoons butter and melt. Cook your mushrooms, celery, and onions in butter till soft.

Add the chicken stock along with the potatoes, then simmer for about 10 minutes.

Then, add your fish to the mixture and cook for another 10 minutes.

Mix in a bowl the flour and clam juice, combine well. Add mixture into the stockpot and let simmer for another few minutes.

Add your seasoning along with salt and pepper, and stir to combine. Remove pot from the heat, and then add in the evaporated milk and stir.

Add fish chowder to serving bowls, then top with crumbled bacon for garnish. Serve hot and enjoy!

Nutrition Information:

- Calories: 386
- Fat: 6
- Carbs: 8
- Cholesterol: 83
- Protein: 9
- Sodium: 748

Caramelized Brussels Sprouts & Pistachios

A healthy recipe that makes for a yummy side dish!

Prep time: 10 minutes

Cook time: 20 minutes

Servings: 8

Ingredients:

- 4 lbs. Brussels sprouts
- 2 tablespoons white sugar
- 4 small red onions, cut into thin strips
- ½ cup butter, unsalted
- ¼ cup red wine vinegar
- sea salt and black ground pepper to taste
- ½ cup pistachios, coarsely chopped

Directions:

Add the Brussels sprouts inside your steamer basket, then place them over a pan of boiling water. Cover and steam your Brussels sprouts for about 10 minutes.

Melt your butter in a deep skillet, add 3 tablespoons vinegar and onions, cook until your onions begin to brown.

Add your Brussels sprouts along with the remaining vinegar and sugar over medium heat. Sauté mixture until lightly caramelized for about 10 minutes.

Season with some salt and pepper to taste, and garnish with pistachios. Serve and enjoy!

Nutrition Information:

- Calories: 271
- Fat: 9
- Carbs: 9
- Cholesterol: 31
- Protein: 9
- Sodium: 93

Italian-Style Baked Orange Roughy

Enjoy this fantastic fish recipe that is full of flavour as well as a healthy meal!

Prep time: 15 minutes

Cook time: 15 minutes

Servings: 4

Ingredients:

- 2 tablespoons Parmesan cheese, grated
- ¼ cup Italian seasoned bread crumbs
- ¼ cup butter, melted
- 1 lb. Orange Roughy fillets
- ¼ teaspoon garlic powder
- 2 tablespoons Romano cheese, grated
- 1 tablespoon parsley, fresh chopped
- sea salt and black ground pepper, to taste

Directions:

Preheat your oven to 400° Fahrenheit. Now, lightly spray a large baking sheet with non-stick cooking spray.

In a bowl, combine the garlic powder, salt, Parmesan cheese, Romano cheese, and breadcrumbs.

Brush both sides of fish fillets with butter, then dredge in breadcrumb mixture.

Place the fillets in one layer on the prepared baking sheet, then drizzle the fillets with parsley.

Bake fillets in the preheated oven for 15 minutes or till fish flakes easily with fork. Serve and enjoy!

Nutrition Information:

- Calories: 242
- Fat: 4
- Carbs: 4
- Cholesterol: 105
- Protein: 9
- Sodium: 645

Blue Cheese Walnut Toasts

A perfect dish to serve at gatherings as a yummy snack!

Prep time: 10 minutes

Cook time: 14 minutes

Servings: 10

Ingredients:

- 4 ounces crumbled blue cheese
- 1 French baguette, sliced into individual slices
- ¼ cup butter, melted
- ¼ cup butter, softened
- ½ cup parsley, chopped
- ½ cup walnuts, chopped
- sea salt and black ground pepper, to taste

Directions:

Preheat your oven to 400° Fahrenheit. Lightly brush your melted butter on one side of the bread, then place it on the baking sheet with the butter side facing up. Bake for seven minutes or till lightly toasted.

Mix the softened butter, blue cheese, pepper, and salt in a small bowl. Spread this mixture on the tops of the toasted bread, then sprinkle walnuts on top.

Bake for about 7 minutes in the oven or until the topping is bubbly and melted. Add to a serving tray and garnish with chopped parsley. Serve and enjoy!

Nutrition Information:

- Calories: 143
- Fat: 8.3
- Carbs: 13.4
- Cholesterol: 16
- Protein: 4.4
- Sodium: 260

Curried Chickpeas

A wonderful chickpea recipe for a perfect lunch meal or side dish for the main meal!

Prep time: 15 minutes

Cook time: 20 minutes

Servings: 6

Ingredients:

- 1 teabag
- 2 cups water
- 2 (15.5 ounces) cans garbanzo beans, drained
- 1 bay leaf
- 2 tablespoons vegetable oil, divided
- 1 onion, sliced
- ¼ cup cilantro leafs, fresh
- 3 tomatoes, diced
- 1 teaspoon cumin seeds
- 1 teaspoon coriander, ground
- 1 teaspoon garlic, grated
- 1 teaspoon ginger root, fresh grated
- 1 teaspoon turmeric, ground
- 1 onion, finely diced
- 1 dash garam masala

Directions:

In a pan, boil 2 cups of water, bay leaf and tea bag. Stir in ½ cup of the garbanzo beans. Once the beans have cooked, remove and discard the teabag and bay leaf. Remove the pan from heat and drain. Set aside and reserve the water.

Heat 2 tablespoons of your vegetable oil, in a skillet over medium heat setting. Sauté the ginger, coriander, garlic, and cumin seeds until light brown or for about 20 seconds. Stir in your turmeric and chopped onion. Cook until onion has softened.

Add to the skillet the remaining tomatoes, season with sea salt, cayenne pepper, and garam masala. Allow the tomato juice to boil and cook for about 5 minutes. Stir in the boiled beans, finely sliced onion, and reserved water.

Continue to cook for an additional 5 minutes, often stirring until consistency thickens. Top with the remaining cilantro leafs. Serve and enjoy!

Nutrition Information:

- Calories: 248
- Fat: 7
- Cholesterol: 0
- Carbs: 2
- Protein: 5
- Sodium: 446

Apple Walnut Salad & Cranberry Vinaigrette Dressing

A light and healthy recipe that will make for a perfect lunchtime meal on a warm day!

Prep time: 20 minutes

Cook time: 10 minutes

Servings: 8

Ingredients:

- 3 Red Delicious apples, cored & thinly sliced
- 8 cups mixed salad greens, rinsed & dried
- 1 cup olive oil
- 1 tablespoon Dijon-style mustard
- 1 cup red onion, thinly sliced
- 1 tablespoon white sugar
- ¼ cup balsamic vinegar
- ½ cup walnuts, chopped
- ¼ cup cranberries

Directions:

First, preheat your oven to 350° Fahrenheit. Spread a single layer of walnuts over a cookie sheet. Place sheet into oven and bake for 10 minutes or until walnuts are slightly toasted.

Combine your mustard, onion, vinegar, sugar, and cranberries in your food processor. Puree mixture until smooth, then slowly pour in the oil, and then season with the salt and pepper.

In a large salad bowl, whisk enough of the cranberry mixture along with sliced apples and greens, toss to coat. Add the salad to serving bowls, then top with some walnuts and enjoy!

Nutrition Information:

- Calories: 24
- Fat: 26
- Carbs: 6
- Protein: 1
- Sodium: 54

Conclusion

I would like to thank you for deciding to download my book of my top Australian and New Zealand recipes! I hope that you will enjoy trying and preparing them as much as I have and still do! I know it is hard for all of us in the world trying to cope with living during the Covid-19 pandemic. It has certainly made more people choose to stay home and stay safe; alas, they cannot travel to countries around the world trying different cuisines as they go! Alas, this cookbook will help give a little taste of some of the famous Australian and New Zealand recipes. Preparing foods from different countries and cultures is thrilling! You can experience new flavours and ways to prepare foods that I am sure you will enjoy! I wish you many days of great enjoyment when sitting down to share a meal with those close to your heart that will give you a little taste of another part of the world!

About the Author

Nancy Silverman is an accomplished chef from Essex, Vermont. Armed with her degree in Nutrition and Food Sciences from the University of Vermont, Nancy has excelled at creating e-books that contain healthy and delicious meals that anyone can make and everyone can enjoy. She improved her cooking skills at the New England Culinary Institute in Montpelier Vermont and she has been working at perfecting her culinary style since graduation. She claims that her life's work is always a work in progress and she only hopes to be an inspiration to aspiring chefs everywhere.

Her greatest joy is cooking in her modern kitchen with her family and creating inspiring and delicious meals. She often says that she has perfected her signature dishes based on her family's critique of each and every one.

Nancy has her own catering company and has also been fortunate enough to be head chef at some of Vermont's most exclusive restaurants. When a friend suggested she share some of her outstanding signature dishes, she decided to add cookbook author to her repertoire of personal achievements. Being a technological savvy woman, she felt the e-book realm would be a better fit and soon she had her first cookbook available online. As of today, Nancy has sold over 1,000 e-books and has shared her culinary experiences and brilliant recipes with people from all over the world! She plans on expanding into self-help books and dietary cookbooks, so stayed tuned!

Author's Afterthoughts

Thank you for making the decision to invest in one of my cookbooks! I cherish all my readers and hope you find joy in preparing these meals as I have.

There are so many books available and I am truly grateful that you decided to buy this one and follow it from beginning to end.

I love hearing from my readers on what they thought of this book and any value they received from reading it. As a personal favor, I would appreciate any feedback you can give in the form of a review on Amazon and please be honest! This kind of support will help others make an informed choice on and will help me tremendously in producing the best quality books possible.

My most heartfelt thanks,

Nancy Silverman

If you're interested in more of my books, be sure to follow my author page on Amazon (can be found on the link Bellow) or scan the QR-Code.

https://www.amazon.com/author/nancy-silverman

Printed in Great Britain
by Amazon

14407812R00045